The Poems

Of

Hattie Parker

Edited by

Barbara Stewart Severson

THE POEMS OF HATTIE PARKER

ISBN 978-0692419410

Comments about Hattie Parker's poems? The editor may be contacted at:

parkerpoetry@mail.com

Foreword

Harriet Rhodes Stewart Parker (known as "Hattie" to her friends and relatives) was born on May 4, 1880, in Pawnee City, Nebraska. In 1899, she married Frank Stewart of Liberty, Nebraska. Their wedding trip was a journey across Nebraska in a covered wagon with her sister and her sister's husband. They traveled for three weeks, looking for a farmstead for a new home, finally settling on a farm seven and a half miles northeast of Beatrice. They had three children, Victor, Gerald, and Eloise, before Frank died of pneumonia in 1916 at the age of 42. In 1920, she married Arda Parker and moved to Princeville, Illinois, where Arda was a telegrapher for the Santa Fe Railroad. They returned to Beatrice in 1940, and Arda died in 1952. Hattie loved reading and making up rhymes, and she was a great collector of articles she found interesting, often pasting them in scrapbooks. At the age of 80, she began to write poetry, and this writing phase lasted through the age of 100. She was a lifelong Methodist, and a 50-year member of the Order of the Eastern Star in Beatrice. She died in her sleep on January 15, 1981, aged 100 years, seven months, and eleven days.

The editor of this book has a special interest in Harriet Parker: She was my great-grandmother!

Table of Contents

Birthdays   **Page**

90th Birthday..8

92nd Birthday...11

93rd Birthday...13

94th Birthday...15

95th Birthday...17

96th Birthday...19

97th Birthday...21

98th Birthday...24

99th Birthday...26

100th Birthday...28

Christmas

Christmas 1974...32

Christmas 1975...34

Christmas Calories...35

Christmas Cards..36

Christmas Cookies...38

Christmas Eve..41

Christmas Treats...42

Day after Christmas..44

Home for Christmas...47

My Interpretation of Christmas..................................50

The Meaning of Christmas.......................................51

Acclamations and Praises

A Tribute to Beatrice, Nebraska.................................52

A Tribute to Johanna... 55

Birthday Wish to a Friend.. 57

Borden's Turnips...58

Golden Wedding..60

My Dog...62

Nellie's Leaving...63

Ode to a New Great-grandson..65

Remembering and Eastern Star Friend..................................67

The Albany Folks...70

Current Events of the Day

A Sad Story about Nixon...72

Forgiving Nixon...75

In Honor of the Bicentennial, 1976..................................78

Nebraska Centennial...81

Nixon and Watergate...88

To the Moon...94

Reflections

Changing Times..98

Exit...100

Friends..102

Life's Highway...104

Life's Laments...105

My Life..109

My Mama..113

My Window..115

Observations...117

Old Age...121

True Riches...123

Tasteless Coffee...127

The Changing World..130

Wistful Thinking..133

Wondering Why...136

Religion and Church

Church Revival...140

Easter...145

Religion Retrospect...146

The Bible...151

The New Church...152

Words of Advice

A Graduate...155

Be Thankful..157

Now is the Time..160

Winning the Race...161

Wise Words..165

Miscellaneous

Flowers and Spring...169

Order of the Eastern Star.......................................171

Pills...175

Birthdays

90th Birthday

I am going to have a birthday,
I will be 90 the 4th of May.
Now that is a lot of living,
No matter what folks say.

Folks say "old age' is golden,
Don't you believe one word.
Of all the things I ever heard,
This is the most absurd.

In case you ever make it,
I just want you to know,
Your body is real achy,
And your feet get very slow.

We get so very weary,
And we don't have much to do.
We try to be contented,
But some days we sit and stew.

We try to grin and take it,

Or to think of something new.
Some days we feel quite frisky,
But those days are very few.

Sometimes we sit and reminisce,
But it doesn't do any good.
You cannot your bring years back,
And you wouldn't if you could.

No, we are just old people,
"Has beens," you might say.
We just sit and fold our hands
And call it another day.

Some days I think perhaps
We were surely born too soon,
And if we live much longer,
We will be wrinkled as a prune.

I'm really not complaining.
Everybody has to die,
But all these aches and miseries,
Why can't they pass us by?

With all my tribulations,
And with all the faults I find,

I am so very thankful
That I do still have my mind.

When Gabriel calls we are ready,
We think He knows the score.
We wouldn't want to keep on living
A hundred years or more.

When we go on from here,
We will call it our gain.
We then will be rested and happy,
And there will be no more pain.

And if the world forgets us,
Who are we to care?
We will be with loved ones,
And there is no night there.

There will be no more birthdays,
Time is not counted by years.
Our troubles will all be over,
Neither will there be any tears.

There is a time to be born, and also a time to die.
We cannot fight our destiny, so we won't even try.

92nd Birthday

Talk about a birthday,
Well I am 92 today.
I never would have believed it,
I'm well along the way.

Don't think you get to be 92
On flowery beds of ease.
I think of many years
Much pleasanter than these.

It's something I never expected,
But I am not a bit dismayed.
I thought that I was wanted,
So that is the reason I stayed.

You all were so nice to me.
You have kept me feeling fine.
If you will only bear with me,
I just might reach 99.

It might not be desirable
And it is not for me to say,
But if I live to be 100,
That will be the day.

But when all is said and done,

It could be much worse.

So with many loving thoughts,

I will send you this little verse.

93rd Birthday

I am having another birthday.
How old, you ask, will I be?
If I can count correctly,
I am going to be 93.

It seems like only yesterday
That I was sweet sixteen.
The world was one big bubble,
And I felt like a queen.

Life hasn't been all pleasure.
There were no two days the same.
But I tried to do my best, and
I always played the game.

I have been in many places,
And I did so many things.
I never was real bad,
But I never sprouted wings.

The Bible says, three score years
Is our allotted time.
Well, I guess I have added
A bonus of 23 years to mine.

Although I'm weary and wrinkled,

And some days full of strife,

I seem to keep on living,

And I still enjoy my life.

Yes, I have had a real long life.

Goodness, mercy me.

I realize I'm a real old woman,

But it is hard to believe I'm 93.

Life can be beautiful,

I know it has been for me.

But it isn't all roses

When you get to be 93.

94th Birthday

Another birthday here again.
Why do they come so fast?
And every year I think,
It will surely be the last.

Time has a way
Of slipping by.
I cannot hold it back,
And why should I try?

I wonder why I'm here,
That I do not know.
I guess it just must be,
That God has willed it so.

If of my greatest joys I speak,
I think of nothing better,
Then when I see the postman,
I know there will be a letter.

A letter from our children
Means a lot when we are old.
When you get into your 90s,
That's old, so I am told.

I am like old machinery
That takes a lot of grease.
It takes a lot of fixing
Before this life will cease.

Lots of pills in the cupboard,
They help and do relieve.
For them you, too, will be thankful,
If the 90s you achieve.

I count a lot on my children,
Come rain or come snow.
When anything goes wrong,
I always let them know.

I hope I'm not a burden,
Hope I'm not in their way.
They make my life so pleasant,
I have half a notion to stay.

95th Birthday

Can it be possible,
That I am 95?
Well the records say that,
As sure as I'm alive.

It has been quite a struggle
As I look back through the years.
Many happy occasions,
But not without tears.

I walk with a cane,
And I have to take care.
But I get where I'm going
Without a wheel chair.

My wrinkles get deeper,
And my body is real saggy.
And I would look better
If my eyes were not baggy.

But time makes these changes.
There is no other way.
As long as we stay here,
That is what we must pay.

I start fresh each morning,
And I just do my best.
But I must say at bed time,
I am sure ready to rest.

I'm sure that my friends
Think I've slipped a gear,
But I don't mind that,
If my mind will stay clear.

Now all of you people
Are well on your way.
Just watch yourself closely,
You, too, may be 95 someday.

96th Birthday

On May 4th, 1976, I have had another year.
That I am worthy of it, is my wish sincere.

Ninety-six years, I hardly can believe,
And not in any way can I one day retrieve.

Our life is like a book, just like a fairy tale,
Some days are good and fair—the next one like a gale!

Some days are smooth sailing, like down a stream we flow.
There comes a gale—we have no sail, our life is ever so.

We all must have a rudder—look about and find you one.
The clouds are all about your, but you must find the sun.

There must be a reason why I have been spared.
I have had all these years of sunshine and all His blessings shared.

We get pretty weary when we can't do our thing,
But God is in the heavens, and the birds still sing.

Life is a serious matter as we live it day by day.
We can never make our goal if we don't watch and pray.

I'm going to keep on trying as I look toward the setting sun.

Till I hear God calling, "Your work on earth is done."

I will do my task each day; I will be reaching for a star.

And when my life is over, He will help me "cross the bar."

97th Birthday

Life keeps going on,
And for strength we look to Heaven.
Finally the day has come,
And I am 97.

Almost a century,
It seems it can't be true.
That I have lived all these years,
It seems like it must be you.

It really is a privilege,
That only comes to a few.
By struggling I have made it.
I hope that you can, too.

For me to be that old,
It just can't be.
If I told you how I felt,
I'd say about 63.

Life is like a book,
Hidden away somewhere.
We wonder with fear and trembling
If our name is written there.

My life now is history,
I lived it day by day.
It takes a lot of patience,
Sometimes you have to pray.

In our later years our friends seem closer
And a little dearer, too.
Among those friends I speak of,
I am including you.

There is a lot of living,
Crowded in these years,
Most of them filled with happiness,
But some days there were tears.

So many of my older friends
Are leaving year by year.
I now have more friends over there,
Than I have over here.

One gets pretty weary
And our feet will hardly go,
When you get to be 97,
You will say "enough" I know.

Soon He is going to call me

To our home "over there."

For Him to say "well done,"

That is now my prayer.

98th Birthday

Please don't ever get old,
It just doesn't pay.
You can't remember things
For longer than a day.

You can't hear what's going on,
Maybe you don't miss much.
It's all about your taxes,
High groceries and such.

Some nights are long and dreary
And you just can't sleep,
So count your blessings
Instead of counting sheep.

When you get to be 80 or 90,
Try to think back when you were small,
Because you really are lucky
If you can think at all.

You change your skates for crutches,
You need a rocking chair.
You change from horse and buggy,
Now you travel in the air.

There is no use griping,
No one is to blame,
But all you need now
Is a wheel chair, crutch and cane.

When all is said and done,
No use to try to shake it.
With a little of God's help,
Your life is what you make it.

When all our work is over,
And when this life ends,
I am looking forward, as
I still will be with friends.

99th Birthday

God has spared me one more year,
It must be he wanted me here.

After all these years that have been mine,
At last I am going to be 99.

I don't want to be bitter,
So I won't be a quitter.

I will keep doing the things I should,
And hope this year will be good.

My feet are so tired and my steps so slow.
It is quite an effort to make them go.

But I'm not giving up, No Sir—ee,
There is too much to do and places to see.

But when my life does end,
I hope someone says, "There goes a friend."

I hope I was a help to someone dear,
Or helped them wipe away a tear.

I hope I eased somebody's pain,
Then my life wasn't lived in vain.

I hope God says, "Now take my hand,
I will lead you to the promised land."

And then I will be with those gone before,
And we will all live together, forevermore!

100th Birthday

It seems almost impossible
That I am 100 years old today.
I hardly can believe it,
But that is what statistics say.

Why that is a whole century,
More than my allotted time.
We all have a destiny,
I guess this must be mine.

Each year since I was 90,
I was sure would be my last.
But each year went by so quickly,
Yes, they passed by so fast.

Some say each year is better,
But that saying isn't true.
Some days you have to
Ask God to help you through.

I wonder where all those years went,
And how all those days were spent.
Did I go that second mile?
Or even help a child to smile?

Time cannot be halted
In this endless flight.
Age is sure to follow,
As the day follows the night.

I have had many joys,
Some days were full of pleasure.
Taking it all in all,
I was blessed without measure.

The road is long
And deep and wide,
But you can make it,
With God on your side.

I never thought much about life,
How long or short it would be.
I just took it day by day,
As it came to me.

I know I made mistakes.
I'm sure I caused some tears.
I hope it is all forgiven
After all these 100 years.

Today if I could change my life

As I write this little verse,
Would I make things better?
Or would I make them worse?

The road has been long and weary,
But I took it day by day.
Our last years are not golden.
Don't believe what people say.

Some days I could hardly make it,
I was so weary and blue.
But I kept trying and praying,
And the sun came shining through.

Life is what you make it,
I'm sure this saying is true.
But there are many stormy places
You have to have help to get through.

These years slipped up on me,
But here I am at last.
Yes I am 100 years old,
I reached my goal at last.

Now I am at the end of the road,
I am headed to the city four square.

There are so many loved ones gone,
And I hope to meet them there.

Christmas

Christmas 1974

Christmas time is here again,
It is time to say, "Ho ho."
Time to get our gloves on,
And go out in the snow.

Lights around our windows,
A wreath is on our door,
Turkey in the icebox,
How could we wish for more?

Everything is so pretty,
Things all decked out in white.
To have it any other color
Would not seem quite right.

We can remember Christmas
When our children were small.
Gifts and candy all around,
And on our tree so tall.

Santa knew them all by name:

Jerry, Vic and Nell.
He knew if they were good or bad,
I wonder how he could tell.

Christmas was so different
Away back then.
We brought all our gifts
At the five and ten.

My children are so far away,
Then cannot come this year.
They wanted to real badly,
But things seemed to interfere.

But I have friends around me;
We can all get together.
That is, I hope we can—
It's depending on the weather.

This Christmas of 1974,
Let us make it better than' 73.
A Merry Christmas one and all
Is the Christmas wish from me.

Christmas 1975

Just yesterday was Christmas.
Today it's a thing of the past.
Everyone is so happy at Christmas,
And how sad it doesn't last.

We look for a new beginning,
A new fresh leaf we turn.
We will do our best as we see it,
And maybe a lesson learn.

And each lesson will help us,
To trudge on as best we can.
At the end of each day, perhaps,
We can be a better man.

And if at the end of 1976,
We can really say we tried,
Let that be enough,
And try to be satisfied.

If I could have one Christmas wish,
I am quite sure it would be,
That everyone in the world
Could be has happy as me.

Christmas Calories

Chicken and dressing
And salads so fine.
To top it all off,
A wee bit of wine.

All kinds of cookies
And pudding and fudge.
The day after Christmas,
I could hardly budge.

I tried all the good things,
And we also had pie.
By the next morning
I could just about die.

Next Christmas I'll watch my calories,
And I will have a better time,
Get up in the morning,
Feeling just fine.

Many children go hungry,
It doesn't seem fair,
For me to sit and stuff,
Just because it's there.

Christmas Cards

This is the day after Christmas,
Many Christmas cards are here.
Most came from a distance,
But a few from around here.

Christmas cards by the dozen.
Yes, some came a long ways.
Each bringing a message
Of those other days.

They make me remember
Some special event,
Of something we did,
Or somewhere we went.

Pictures of the grandchildren
Came by the score,
And believe it or not,
Each year there are more.

But each one is special
In its own way.
I would have them live closer
If I could have my way.

But I am thankful for pictures
And letters and such,
And to all those who sent them,
Thanks very much.

Christmas Cookies

Cookies, cookies everywhere,
On plates and in my dishes.
I see them everywhere,
Some shapes that look like fishes.

Cookies, cookies, who said cookies?
I sure have them now, galore.
When they are all eaten,
Please send me some more.

When do I like cookies?
Morning, noon and night.
That is pretty often,
But, by gum, that is right.

Yes, I do like cookies,
But afraid right now I'm stuck.
You really sent me cookies,
Enough to fill a truck.

Yes, I'll be full of cookies
Like my eyes are full of tears.
I see them all around me,
Even sticking out my ears.

Now, Scott*, why did you let her*
Send me so many cans?
They fill up all my dishes,
And all my pots and pans.

You are a little rascal.
I bet you laughed and said,
When Grandma eats all those,
I'm sure she will be dead.

Now, thank you a million,
Yes, and even more.
But now my dear darling,
Please don't send me anymore.

If you think sending so many
Was a really good joke,
I'm going to eat them, every one,
And then I'm going to croak.

So goodbye, now I am no more,
I am just a rookie.
You have no Grandma Hattie now,
I've turned into a cookie.

So bury me out on the hill,

Where they bury all the rookies.
Instead of flowers on my grave,
Just pile it high with cookies.

I think I am in Heaven now
Where angels live on love.
I'm glad I had my cookies here.
There won't be any up above.

*Hattie's great-grandson and granddaughter-in-law.

Christmas Eve

'Tis the day before Christmas
And all through the house,
Nothing is happening,
I haven't even a spouse.

My gifts are all lying out on the bed,
From shoes for my feet to a scarf for my head.
Fruit, nuts and cookies all came from the west,
While gloves, hose and dishes came from the rest.

If wishes came true,
You all would be here.
It's sad to have Christmas
And no children near.

But if you are happy
And doing your best,
I will leave you to God,
And let Him do the rest.

This year is about over,
And what did we learn?
But the year coming up
Is our greatest concern.

Christmas Treats

Well I got some jelly
And I got some honey.
It came in the mail,
Didn't cost me any money.

The mailman left it
As he went down the street,
And I am real sure
It will be quite a treat.

What is better for breakfast
Than bread, butter, and jam?
And I always eat it,
Is why I'm as well as I am.

So thank you my dears,
What more can I say?
I will be thinking of you
As I eat it each day.

It will be good on biscuits,
And pancakes, too.
When I'm eating it
I will sure think of you.

Come over some day,
We will eat it together
And you better hurry
On account of the weather.

Day after Christmas

Well Christmas is over,
It was a very nice day.
Santa came as usual,
But not in a sleigh.

Because we didn't have snow,
And we didn't have rain,
So I think this year,
That he came on a train.

He brought several things,
But it wasn't enough.
It was just cookies and apples
And all that kind of stuff.

Yes, the day after Christmas,
I have things galore.
But I'm never satisfied,
I always want more.

I asked for a typewriter
I thought I could use,
But instead of that,
He brought me new shoes.

I asked for a freezer,
I thought would be handy.
I didn't get that,
Just a small sack of candy.

I see nice things in windows,
Someone gets them I guess.
I'd like a new purse
And a pretty new dress.

I wanted a bicycle
So I wouldn't have to walk.
He brought me a slate,
And a long piece of chalk.

I asked for so much,
I guess I made him mad.
So now I have to do
With the things I already had.

I guess I shouldn't complain,
I suppose he brought me enough,
If it had been what I wanted,
Instead of apples and stuff.

Santa thought because I'm old

I didn't need much,
So he brought me a shawl,
And a cane and a crutch.

Yes, I'm a Scrooge at Christmas,
It really is a shame.
If I didn't get one thing,
I'd have myself to blame.

So in 1973 I will try,
To change my point of view,
And maybe by next Christmas
I will be happy like you.

Home for Christmas

I think I will go home for Christmas,
I really think I should.
I haven't been there lately,
And the old folks aren't too good.

I write them real often,
No matter where I roam.
I tell them that I love them,
But that's not like going home.

I remember mother's table.
It was always set for four.
We filled up on all her good things,
Till we could eat no more.

But especially on Christmas,
Things had a brighter look.
She gathered things together
And showed how she could cook.

The cranberries were so pretty,
The mince pie tasted like it should.
Seemed like the whole table
Was filled with everything good.

Such a fine Christmas dinner,
The turkey was so good.
The dressing and all the trimmings,
We all ate more than we should.

We talked about our old times
And how things used to be,
And how everything was decorated,
Even our Christmas tree.

The neighbors' tree was bigger,
And it had more fancy stuff.
But we seemed to be contented, as
We always had enough.

Sometimes we didn't have turkey,
A chicken had to do.
But mother knew how to fix it,
Somehow into a stew.

Our Christmases were merry,
No matter what we had.
Since then I have not seen better,
But those were not so bad.

Yes I better fly home for Christmas,

And stay a day or two,

And see how things are doing,

Maybe there is something I could do.

My Interpretation of Christmas

C—Is for Christmas, best day of the year.

If we believe this we have nothing to fear.

H—Is for Him, whose birthday we keep,

And it is in Him whose guidance we seek.

R—Is for Righteous, we know that He is,

And if we obey Him we all can be His.

I—Is for Intentions, either good or bad.

One makes us happy, the other sad.

S —Is for Someone who cares for you.

He keeps you happy, honest and true.

T—Is for Triumph over wrong and sin.

Christmas is the very best day to begin.

M—Is for Master and savior and friend.

How badly we need Him when we come to the end.

A—Is for Angels with Him up above.

We all can be angels if Him we will love.

S—Is for Shepherd the guarder of sheep.

He has promised to watch us while we are asleep.

Yes the birthday of Jesus, the Christ child we love.

He sends all our blessings, down from above.

Let's keep it sacred, and not desecrate,

And He will meet us at the Golden Gate.

The Meaning of Christmas

What does Christmas mean to you?
It means a lot to me.
It is our most Holy day, and
Means more than a Christmas tree.

It means the birthday of a Savior,
Bringing to us good will.
He ever has loved and blessed us,
And He is with us still.

He wants us to be happy,
But He also wants us good.
It is easy to be both
If we worship as we should.

He is the King of Kings,
Whose birthday now we keep.
So let us bow before Him,
And all His blessings seek.

As we gather with loved ones,
And with all the Christmas fuss,
Let us all remember
To invite Him to be with us.

Acclamations and Praises

A Tribute to Beatrice, Nebraska

Are you looking for a new location?
Are you planning to build or buy?
Before you go any further,
Give Beatrice a try.

We have what you are looking for;
We have many pretty spots.
We have places built already,
And many desirable lots.

We have places on the river
And some nice ones on a hill.
Anything you are looking for,
Beatrice can fill the bill.

There are beautiful homes to look at,
And fine lots to look at, too.
In almost any direction,
There is a lovely view.

People come here as strangers,

They have been on the road.
But when they see Beatrice,
They soon buy themselves a home.

Our town is up and coming,
It's a lively little place.
Our churches and our schools
Are far from a disgrace.

Our city is the bestest,
Reserved, genteel, not loud.
It is called "the city of churches,"
Of this we are real proud.

We have beautiful trees and flowers,
And a river runs through our town.
Our fine schools and churches,
Make it a city of renown.

Even our weather is perfect.
It is neither cold nor hot,
So if you are looking for a location,
Beatrice is sure the spot.

I am satisfied with Beatrice,
After sixty years all told.

Hope to stay here a little longer,
Although I'm getting pretty old.

I may not be a poet,
But in real estate perhaps.
Telling people about our city,
Helps put Beatrice on the map.

A Tribute to Johanna

Her real name is Johanna.
We call her Anna for short.
When you get to know her,
She is a real sport.

She is gracious to others.
She has been kind to me.
She is always friendly.
She is as nice as she can be.

She comes and takes me to dinner,
In my wheel chair.
You never have to worry.
You know she's always there.

Let's all be kind to Anna,
And when all is said and done,
May she be on the side that wins,
When the race is run.

We are like one family,
We have to give and take.
We have to watch our manners,
For the other's sake.

She seems to like everybody,

And they like her, too.

We must be congenial,

Me and her and you.

And when life is over,

And we are all up there,

May we all be together,

So she can push my chair.

---written at age 100 for an employee of the Good Samaritan Center, Beatrice

Birthday wish to a friend

I heard you had a birthday,
And if that is true,
I will have to admit
That I had forgotten you.

Birthdays come so often,
Time goes by so fast,
Seems like just a week ago
That you had your last.

I hope you had a good day.
I hope my wish isn't late.
I sure hope someone
Baked you a real big cake.

And as you live from year to year,
And to your own self be true,
May you have many friends,
And may God be good to you.

And when birthdays are over,
And time for us ends,
I think that we
Will still be friends.

Borden's Turnips

Folks all know that you garden.
But some things they don't know.
It takes a lot of patience,
And hard work with a hoe.

There is a method to a garden,
Just when to spade and seed.
If it is done correctly,
You never will see a weed.

I want to speak of your turnips.
They were so very nice.
I separated mine,
So I could cook some twice.

Some folks can't raise them,
And some folks won't try.
Many folks enjoyed yours,
And one of them was I.

You spend lots of time in your garden,
And if what I hear is true,
Half the people up there
Are living off of you.

That doesn't seem fair,
But you are a good scout,
The kind of a neighbor
Folks can't live without.

If you raise turnips next year,
That will suit me fine.
Along about November
I will come back for mine.

I hear you like to pick berries,
So you planted quite a few.
Now is this a hillside joke?
Or is it really true?

I guess it makes you happy,
To give so much away.
God loves a cheerful giver,
So that's where you get your pay.

I could go on and on and on,
But I think this is enough.
You must be tired of reading
All this silly rhyming stuff.

Golden Wedding

A golden wedding is a privilege
That comes to a very few,
So thank your Heavenly Father
That is has come to you.

You have had fifty years together,
That is a very long time.
Some days were very rough,
And some days things were fine.

It takes a lot of courage
And a lot of patience, too.
There was lots of work and trouble,
And sorrow to go through.

But things can be accomplished
If you both work hand in hand,
And each one thinks the other
Is the finest in the land.

The obstacles are many,
But all of them you won.
Some were heavy burdens,
They seemed just like a ton.

God sent along a family,
You did your very best.
You put them in God's hands,
And He did all the rest.

Of your children you are very proud;
They are worth much more than gold.
And each one was a blessing
As it came into the fold.

Through thick and thin you managed,
Discouraged, tired and blue.
As you look back, you know
It was Him who helped you through.

------written for son Victor and his wife in 1967

My Dog

A nice little dog, with cute little ears,
I've wanted so much, for many long years.

You see I didn't want just any old kind,
And what I wanted, I just couldn't find.

I didn't want a cross dog, or one that would bite.
I knew someday I'd find one just right.

Some were too big, and some too small.
I wanted what I wanted, or wanted none at all.

It is hard to believe I now have a pup.
I will teach it tricks, and how to stand up.

It is really a dandy, as cute as can be.
I sure love it, and it loves me.

I now have a real pal; we can go for a jog.
I love it a lot, my sweet little dog.

If my back gets lame, if it slips a cog,
It will surely be caused by long walks with my dog.

Nellie's Leaving

Nellie is going to leave us.
It makes us all real sad.
But if her life in St. Joe is pleasant,
Then we will all be glad.

We all have learned to love her,
And we hate to see her go.
But life is ever changing.
It seems that it is so.

She is always up and ready,
To play us a dandy game.
With someone else in her place,
It never will be the same.

She was a wonderful hostess.
We never can forget that.
As around her bountiful table,
We so often sat to chat.

We never will forget her.
She has a place in our heart.
Don't know when it got there,
Guess it was from the start.

Yes Nellie, we all love you.

You have been to us all a pal.

The way you entertained us,

You really are quite a gal.

Gone but not forgotten,

Every time we play together.

We will always think of you,

Regardless of the weather.

So think of us kindly.

We will think of you the same.

The way we play our cards,

Is the way we play life's game.

--------Written for friend Nellie F, who was moving from Beatrice to St. Joseph, Missouri.

Ode to a New Great-great-grandson

God sent us a little angel
To live with us a while.
He is a little darling.
You ought to see him smile.

He cries and smiles and wiggles,
And sometimes makes a fuss.
But we don't mind the trouble.
We are so glad he came to us.

Day by day he gets sweeter.
He is wrapped around our heart.
He has been very precious,
Right from the very start.

Proud to think he is ours.
It's almost too good to be true.
He is just a little darling,
When he smiles at you.

We will do our best to raise him
Into a God-fearing man.
And with God's help and prayer,
We really think we can.

Yes, he is very special.

Life will never be sad.

If all through life he remembers,

To love his Mom and Dad.

Remembering an Eastern Star Friend

She has gone and cannot be with us.
We cannot see her more,
But we know that she is waiting
For us on the other shore.

Gone but not forgotten,
We think of her each day.
For her to go before us,
Seemed to be His way.

Once again the Lord has spoken.
He has said, "Come unto me."
She answered, "Lord I'm ready,"
To live in Heaven with Thee.

So she has only left us
For that world that is so fair.
Let us follow in her footsteps,
And hope to meet her there.

His house is well illumined,
The streets are paved with gold.
We will know each other better,
In our Bible, that's what we're told.

Yes, that house is waiting for us.

Who will be next we cannot say.

But we will live forever,

If we will but watch and pray.

In His house are many.

This He tells us o'er and o'er.

So one by one He takes us,

To dwell forever more.

He says, "Come unto me, ye weary,

And I will give you rest."

So put your trust in Jesus,

And He will do what is best.

So goodbye, our dear sister.

The Lord had need of thee.

Now let us all be faithful,

Until His face we see.

This world is only for a time,

Given to us to prepare,

For a long and a better life,

With loved ones over there.

In that land that is fairer than day,

A home we all will share:

The good and the true and the faithful,

And there is no night there.

We all should stop and listen,

And for His love aspire.

Someday, and before too long,

He will bid us come up higher.

And when we hear Him call us,

May our lamps be trimmed and bright,

And he will gather us to Him,

And everything will be all right.

Yes, she has gone to her Heavenly Father,

To that land so fair and far.

But we feel her presence with us,

She is still an Eastern Star.*

*See poem on page 172.

The Albany Folks

There is a nice bunch of people,
Who live on a special hill,
In a quaint little town,
Name it if you will.

The river is nearby,
Such a pretty hue.
Every time you look,
You see a different view.

The sunsets are gorgeous
As they sink in the west.
They reflect on the water,
And God does the rest.

These folks are so congenial,
And such jolly people, too.
They get together often
And find nice things to do.

They have real fun upon the hill,
Suppers and dinners and such.
They may even have breakfasts.
It wouldn't surprise me much.

There are the Crockers and the Stewarts,
Bordens and Clara Ruth,
Dolans, Bessie Beach and others.
This is all the truth.

Yes, a special little hill
In this certain little town.
This group of people,
In this town are renowned.

There couldn't be a finer group,
Or I guess a finer hill.
When it comes to good people to know,
They really fit the bill!

Current Events of the Day

A Sad Story about Nixon

Just a few lines about Nixon,
And his fall from grace.
Someone will have to take over,
Someone must fill his place.

As I write these lines about him,
It almost breaks my heart.
He has made such a miserable failure
From such a promising start.

He thinks he is so mighty.
He thinks he is so great.
We think he is so crooked
And has no way to escape.

Each day the plot thickens,
Things we hardly can believe.
Now it is tapes he has tampered with
And is trying to retrieve.

He had trouble with his appointees

As fast as they were hired.
One big mistake he made
Was when he caused Cox* to be fired.

One mistake after another.
He seems to be disturbed.
What he wants us to believe,
It really is absurd.

It gets worse with each newscast,
Our papers are full of mistrust.
To bring things to a climax,
We people really must.

He is so much like Hitler.
He thinks he knows it all,
But he better remember,
The mighty can take a fall.

He really has had a tumble
And he may end up in jail.
Then he will want us dumbbells
To come and make his bail.

It's up to us, it's our country,
And he is so full of deceit.

Somebody has to do something.

Or we will go down in defeat.

Impeachment now is the question,

With which we have to deal

Either that or he resigns,

Is the way the people feel.

It's too late, he can't change us.

Now we are somewhat wiser.

We elected him to be president

And we do not want a Kaiser.

------Written on November 11, 1973

*Watergate Special Prosecutor Archibald Cox, who was fired by President Nixon on October 20, 1973.

Forgiving Nixon

Well all this forgiveness
Is not my kind.
The people in this country
Are not all blind.

A lie is a lie,
And taxes are not free.
The president should pay them,
The same as you and me.

If we lied about our taxes,
Three homes and a tape,
There would be no mercy,
We could not escape.

Now what if it were you,
And what if it were me?
Do you think for a minute,
That we could go free?

You know it's all wrong,
It has to be.
For his helpers are in jail,
And he can go free.

Where is there any justice?
I'd like to know.
If our government has any,
It doesn't show.

People are pretty mad
About this deal.
It will take a long time,
For feelings to heal.

If I were a man,
I sure would fight.
I would do all I could,
To set things right.

Laws are broken
From day to day.
The rich go free
And the poor must pay.

There has to be justice,
Or our laws won't last.
They better correct them,
And do it real fast.

Yes, there must be justice.

Did President Ford do right?
Or should we all get together,
And put up a big fight?

In Honor of the Bicentennial, 1976

Two hundred years ago, our forefathers
Crossed the ocean wide.
They wanted to try their luck
Over on this side.

They soon ran into troubles,
To discourage any man.
But they all got together,
And they began to plan.

They agreed to work together,
And all do their very best.
The rain and sun and weather
Seemed to do the rest.

They dug and plowed and planted.
They fought both drought and snow.
They worked from dawn to sunset,
But progress was very slow.

They had many hardships.
The days were hot and long.
The land was very cheap.
They bought it for a song.

78

They built themselves little cabins,
And dug themselves a well.
They bought themselves some cattle,
Fed them till they were fit to sell.

Although they seemed to prosper,
They had hardships all the way.
One day they got discouraged
And they began to pray.

Praying was their answer.
Prosperity loomed ahead.
They now saw their families,
And livestock could be fed.

Next they built schools and churches,
Of this they saw the need.
Religion they must have,
No matter what the creed.

Education meant more freedom.
That's what they were working for.
After years of struggle,
Success came to their door.

Thus, it was our ancestors,

We call them "pioneers,"
That made this country great,
But it took two hundred years.

Yes, they had many struggles,
But they were staunch and true.
That is why we today
Have the red, white, and blue.

But the flag is worth the effort,
With reverence we hold it high.
We are proud of our stars and stripes,
And for it we all would die.

Nebraska Centennial

Andrew Johnson was our president
When Nebraska became a state.
We tried to make it sooner,
But for red tape we had to wait.

We were the 17th state to join,
And others entered fast.
The last I heard there were fifty,
And Hawaii was the last.

At that time it was call the Union,
And most were territories then.
To get them all united
Took many dedicated men.

And so another star
Went in our lovely flag,
And for this lovely emblem
We have a right to brag.

Ninety-three counties make our state,
They differ much in size.
But for wheat and corn and milo,
Gage County takes the prize.

Butler was Nebraska's first governor.

People called him Dave.

He was a very good executive,

But he always needed a shave.

I will not go into politics,

But will sneak in this one word:

Nebraska is Republican,

Majority about one-third.

Omaha is our largest city,

But others are growing fast.

Nebraska is really booming,

We hope that it will last.

Our state capitol in is Lincoln,

The governor's mansion, too.

If anyone is interested,

Someone will take you through.

Also our state penitentiary,

It had to be somewhere,

And any who are imprisoned,

It's their own fault they are there.

Our governor's name is Tiemann,*

And after quite a fight,

He seems to be real busy,

We think he'll be all right.

There are bound to be some problems,

He is a man of great renown.

I'm sure he will get our votes again

If he keeps our taxes down.

Goldenrod is our state flower,

For years it has been so.

You couldn't find a nicer one,

No matter where you would go.

The only state with a unicameral,

With which to make our laws.

Whether this way is worse or better,

Makes one stop and pause.

To live in Nebraska is a heritage,

And proud we will always be.

We are never taxed too heavily,

But there is a sales tax for you and me.

We are sometimes called the Arbor State,

And we celebrate Arbor Day.

It is because we all plant trees
Along our state highway.

So this is our Centennial year,
Nebraska is 100 years old.
To say it is the best in the Union,
Would be a statement bold.

It once belonged to the Indians,
Or at least that is what folks say.
They tramped the hills and prairies,
And lived here many a day.

They shot quail for a living,
And fished in the Big Blue.
When they got real hungry,
They shot a deer or two.

They thought they were settled forever,
But the white man came along.
He dickered for their possessions,
And got it all for a song.

The white men started farming,
And with just a few odd tools.
They started digging and planting.

They also started schools.

The land was rough and rugged,
They tried to raise some grain.
The winds were hot and heavy,
And they prayed for rain.

Corn was their main product,
I think they called it maize.
They didn't make much of a living,
Prices were cheap in those days.

But they kept struggling on,
Each year more settlers came.
They toiled and worked and sweat and ached,
But each harvest had no gain.

Then one day Dan Freeman** came.
He didn't want to room.
He wanted a place to settle down,
And have himself a home.

And so he went to the government
And got himself a claim.
He settled on a great big ranch,
And there he did remain.

He built a hut and settled down,
Now these were better days.
He tilled the soil and got a crop,
And a big family he did raise.

They called his place a homestead,
The first in the USA,
So it became quite prominent
And still is to this day.

Now it is National Monument Park,
Of which we are very proud.
Each year it brings more people,
Some days there is quite a crowd.

Our capitol building proudly stands
With its stately steeple of gold.
It is not surpassed in all our states,
And it is beautiful to behold.

Nebraska is noted for education.
Our colleges are the very best.
If anyone should doubt it,
Just put it to the test.

Our churches, too, are many,

Of every creed and kind,

And always full on Sunday,

As packed as you can find.

Our jails are always empty,

We all obey the law.

As a whole state taken together,

We are the best you ever saw.

No other state is quite like ours,

From Texas to Alaska.

So all join in and help us say,

"GOD BLESS GOOD OLD NEBRASKA!"

*Norbert Tiemann was Nebraska's governor from 1967-1971.

**An early Nebraska pioneer who, in 1863, submitted the first claim under Lincoln's Homestead Act.

Nixon and Watergate

This story I am about to relate
Is very sad, about Nixon and Watergate.

Richard Milhous Nixon,
What an illustrious name.
He counts on that a little
To help him play the game.

He has a real nice family;
They have helped him quite a bit.
Things went well for quite a while,
Then he began to slip.

He hired the wrong people
To help him do his work.
He turned things over to them,
And they began to shirk.

To skip all over the country,
To Russia and Japan,
He had some talks with Khrushchev,
And with Pompidou man to man.

He seems to be quite gracious,

Smart and capable, too.
He promised so many things
That he was going to do.

That secret grain sale to Russia
Was really a dirty deal.
Talk to most any farmer,
They will tell you how they feel.

He wants everything so secret,
Yes, he surely is "tricky Dick."
He will take us down the drain
If folks don't begin to kick.

I think he is in trouble,
That takes him down a notch or two,
It puts him on a level
With folks like me and you.

He was so afraid McGovern*
Would bring our country to ruin.
He didn't do any better,
Look what he is a doin'.

We should have voted for McGovern,
It would have been a change.

We would have voted for him,
But Nixon told us he was strange.

Better to be strange than crooked,
I'd rather be in McGovern's shoes,
Than to have to face the media
Every day in Watergate news.

"Peace with honor,"
We so often heard him say.
We finally got the "peace,"
But where is his honor today?

We hear him talk on TV,
Talks both early and late.
Keeps us informed on everything,
But he won't mention "Watergate."

Closed doors and secret sessions
Are Nixon's chief delights,
Wanting things so secret,
Hasn't been so bright.

Seems like we can't believe him,
I think it is too bad.
He seems to be the oddest

President we've ever had.

Some of his friends are in trouble:
Ehrlichman, Haldeman and Dean.**
They all seem to be hiding,
At least they are never seen.

Nixon appointed two "plumbers:"
Gordon Liddy and Howard Hunt.***
They broke into Ellsberg's office,****
What an awful stunt.

Camp David he calls home,
And Key Biscayne he likes, too,
To spend a week at the White House
Would be something new.

So many homes he seems to have,
And people think it funny.
At least one of them we know
Was bought with election money.

The sneaky things that he has done,
And the promises he broke,
It really is a wonder
It doesn't make you choke.

People are not so dumb,
One thing we were taught:
The crooked and deceitful
Eventually will get caught.

Someone made a boo boo,
Down there at Watergate.
You know he should have stopped it,
But now it is too late.

Now wouldn't it be awful,
If Dick was asked to resign,
And Agnew would be president
Because he is next in line.

What a pity it all happened,
You never can live it down.
Several will be imprisoned,
And all were so renowned.

When this all is settled,
And the race is run.
The Democrats will be in the White House
Having all that fun.

He will be out of the picture,

And no one will care a mite.
We will see less and less of him,
Eventually he will be out of sight.

When all the court hearings are over,
And all his efforts fail,
His pals will all be with him,
They all will be in jail.

We pray God will forgive him,
But whether He will or not,
He put yourself and family
In a pretty dirty spot.

Now this winds up my story,
I think it is enough.
You asked for a poem about Nixon,
And I have called your bluff.

*South Dakota Senator George McGovern, Nixon's opponent in the 1972 presidential election.
**Nixon aides John Erhlichman, H R Haldeman, and John Dean.
***American intelligence officers implicated in the Watergate break in.
****Military analyst Daniel Ellsberg.

To the Moon: July 20, 1969

Our three brave astronauts,
With courage almost complete,
Trained themselves for a journey,
The man in the moon to meet.

They strapped themselves in Apollo,
High up in the Heavens they went.
And higher and higher they soared,
Faster was their intent.

The three wives reluctantly said,
"We consent, so go if you must.
We will be anxiously waiting,
And in God we will trust."

We all were very fearful,
As they settled in Apollo Eleven.
Seemed to people here below,
They were almost into Heaven.

But on and on they traveled.
Yes, on and on they sailed.
They were determined to get there,
Unless something failed.

With faith in the elements
And faith in their ship,
Onward and upward,
It was an adventurous trip.

They sure have made history,
Beyond any doubt.
But did they really know
How it would all turn out?

They all left their families
To make history for us,
And what they accomplished
Has made history plus!

They talked on the phone,
And we heard it down here.
We all were so worried,
But they seemed to have no fear.

They sent lots of pictures.
They had plenty of food.
They tended to business,
And slept when in the mood.

This all is something unheard of,

In all our world before.

But this is only a starter.

There will be so much more.

Some folks think it all foolish,

But scientists say, "Not so."

To know what is all around us,

The world has been far too slow.

This all is a big step forward,

But that money could all be used,

To help the poor and underprivileged,

Who think they are abused.

Yes, it took a pile of money,

But Uncle Sam didn't seem to care.

He wanted to prove a theory,

That man can't live up there.

Some say, why not be contented,

And leave things as before.

Let us not go to the moon,

We need money for the war.

This all is so inspiring,

But more is coming soon.

Hurrah for the USA!
Now our flag is on the moon!

Hurrah for Apollo Eleven,
And all three men aboard.
It was a dangerous journey,
But the victory they scored.

In 15 days the Apollo returned
And splashed down in the ocean.
A blimp above and boats right near,
It caused a big commotion.

All hail to our venturesome astronauts,
The great, the brave and the strong.
Armstrong, Aldrin and Collins,
Much glory to them belongs.

And now the nation celebrates,
In cities great and small.
But they are most deserving.
They are entitled to it all.

Reflections

Changing Times

Our times are changing
From day to day,
People seem to care less
What they do and say.

Our first years were better,
I think more people were good.
They cared more for others,
And I think people should.

These last few years, it seems
People like to quarrel.
No one is contented,
So many are immoral.

If we just could go back
To those good old days,
To the old-fashioned clothing
And the old-fashioned ways.

Where the woman wore dresses

And the men wore the pants,
And the children were courteous,
But there isn't much chance.

The talk of the day is pills and sex,
It's even in all the papers.
And no one seem to care
About our young folks' capers.

Clothing is no problem,
The less they have on the better.
They like to have it bare
Clear down to their setter.

So I say alas and alack,
Young people have no shame.
Where they go and what they do,
I think parents are to blame.

I speak of kids in general,
I really don't mean **mine**,
Because I did a better job—
My kids all turned out fine!

Exit

My life is nearly over.
I will go to that other home.
It's just across the river, and
I will not be alone.

So many friends before me,
Are waiting there, I know,
And you will soon be coming
In a few short years or so.

This life has been quite lovely,
But many heartaches, too.
Some just came naturally,
And some were caused by you.

When I leave this earth,
And when I cross the bar,
I have to go it all in faith,
I cannot see that far.

Again we will be one family,
Not even one empty chair.
We all will be real happy,
And there will be no night there.

I'm going to my home in Heaven,

That city four square.

According to the Bible,

I will meet you over there.

Friends

A friend is very hard to get,
And harder still to keep.
And so to lose a good one,
Is bound to make you weep.

No one has too many,
Much gold is each one worth.
If we have plenty of them,
We are the richest folks on earth.

Just a pat on the shoulder,
Sometimes does quite a lot.
To help someone take courage,
Where otherwise they would not.

There is always someone watching,
No matter what you do.
So do not fail to watch your words,
And to your friends be true.

It's the little things in life that count,
So lend a helping hand.
It will help at least someone
To better understand.

A kind word softly spoken,
With no effort on your part,
Will start someone rejoicing
Or mend a broken heart.

There is sorrow all around us,
Things we cannot see.
Folks who are sad and weary,
That could be helped by you and me.

So let us be up and doing,
Let us work with all our might,
And we will see around us
Many things that are not right.

Life flies by so swiftly,
We even neglect our own.
Let us try to be more loving,
And not have a heart of stone.

What can we do about it?
That is not for me to say.
But this, I know will help a lot,
If we will only pray.

Life's Highway

As you travel down life's highway,
May you meet life with a smile.
As you come to all the crossroads,
May things get brighter every mile.

May all your troubles be behind you,
And good luck not pass you by.
You will find life worth living,
Your part is just to try.

It's just as easy to see sunshine,
As to see clouds on a rainy day.
If you look through rose-colored glasses,
Everything is bright, not gray.

So look up and keep on smiling.
You are one of God's chosen few.
We are wishing, hoping, praying,
Nothing but the best for you.

Life's Laments

My life has been so different
Than I ever intended.
I had so much planned,
And now it is almost ended.

I intended so much to travel.
There is so much to see,
And there are so many wonders,
And so many of them free.

The seas and the oceans,
With their big billowy waves.
They say there is great beauty
In our big mammoth caves.

One great wonder to see
Is the big Boulder Dam,
That and many others
Given by our good Uncle Sam.

Another thing I wanted to do
Was to go to Washington for a day or two.
Stay in a hotel and live in style,
And stay a few days and rest a while.

Our nation's capitol
Is a sight we should see,
And no one ever wanted to,
Any more than me.

I wanted to go to Canada
Just to see my aunt Nell.
She was such a nice person,
But she was never well.

Another thing I wanted
Was to see the Atlantic Ocean,
But seems things at home
Were in a great commotion.

Sometimes I thought I wanted fame,
To have a couple letters after my name,
But I would sit and contemplate,
Instead of studying early and late.

I kept thinking I'd do it next year.
First thing I knew, that year was here.
Time slipped by in a peculiar way,
And I kept busy, from day to day.

I would like to go to Paris,

Perhaps buy myself a home.
I would like to see Queen Elizabeth,
And also the Pope of Rome.

I thought of going to Mexico
And see some of the south.
The year I planned that,
Was the year we had our drought.

Yes, I so wanted to travel,
By car and boat and train
But I never did hanker
To go any place by plane.

Why didn't I get busy
And do all those things so nice?
I had the time and money
Could have even seen them twice.

So many disappointments
In this life I have had,
And as I look backward
It really makes me sad.

So please live for today.
Don't wait for tomorrow.

It will only bring you
Discomfort and sorrow.

Now as I sit and ponder,
Why did I procrastinate,
And cry upon your shoulder,
Now that it is too late?

I still have one more journey,
That one I haven't forgot.
It is on a picturesque landscape
In a beautiful six foot plot.

When all your journeys are ended,
And you are free from care,
When all life's duties are transacted
Come rest beside me there.

Thus the chapter is ended
And if I have done my best,
Whether I traveled or didn't,
God will do the rest.

My Life

How times have changed since 1880,
The beginning of my life.
I came into this world so small,
Into a world full of strife.

A sister five and a brother three,
Greeted me right away.
They looked me over well
And wanted me to stay.

My parents, too, seemed concerned
And hoped I'd be real good.
In a baby's way of talking,
I promised them I would.

One by one the years went by,
Unmeaningful and slow.
What life was all about,
I didn't really know.

I wondered what my life would be,
With God's help, no doubt.
And would I be responsible for
The way it all turned out?

Well life went on, year after year.

With each came joy and sorrow.

And faith and hopes and fears,

Each day like the tomorrow.

Life is like a school.

Each day we have a task.

For this we need some help,

We get it if we ask.

As years slip by,

Our problems double,

And all around us,

We see folks in trouble.

Some folks long for riches,

Others reach for fame.

Neither one is so important,

But it's how you play the game.

I never accomplished much in life,

As some of you have done.

But this I know: it's been worthwhile

Because I raised a son.

Yes, two sons and a daughter,

In time were sent to me,
Making life worthwhile,
As all lives ought to be.

To raise three children
Is quite a task.
You need some guidance
And for this you ask.

And even then with extra help
It gets a little tough.
The way looks dark,
And the going gets rough.

The whole way through,
Really it isn't very funny.
It takes a lot of patience,
And quite a lot of money.

Time seems to pass, and
The children roam.
They all grow up.
Soon, they all leave home.

That is the way you want it.
There is really no use to moan.

But after all these years,
You now are left alone.

Some go east and some go west,
Out into the great unknown.
That was the way intended,
For each to have their home.

But all is well as I sit alone,
Cold and feeble and grey.
Life has been good through it all,
I would have it no other way.

Now I'm trudging on,
To the very last.
My faith and love
Are holding fast.

My Mama

When I was a little bitty baby,
My mama said to me,
You have come into a world
Where everything is free.

Yes, free for your own choosing,
So be careful, choose with care.
There are signs that say enter,
And signs that say beware.

My mama told me many things,
She also told me this:
Bad folks' life is full of trouble
But good folks' life is bliss.

Speak gently or do not speak at all,
And never do be loud.
Keep your manners humble, and
No one likes the proud.

She said friends are watching,
As we come and go.
We are their example
When we don't even know.

Once she told me what you sew,
You will also reap,
And one thing real important
Is the company you keep.

My mama often warned me
Of the pitfalls along the way.
Try to be kind and helpful,
And be careful what you say.

So I try to always remember
All the good things that she said.
Her loving hands still guide me,
Although she is a long time dead.

My Window

I see from my window
The beautiful sky,
And clouds and birds,
And traffic going by.

I see from my window
A beautiful day,
All nature in splendor
And nothing to pay.

I see from my window
A child out at play,
I'm sure he is having
A real happy day.

I see from my window
A church with a steeple,
A crowd going in,
They look like happy people.

I see from my window
A beautiful sight,
The moon coming up,
And the stars are so bright.

As I look out my window
I see a gentle rain.
It greens up the grass
And ripens the grain.

As I look out my window
I see a sweet child.
I wave my hand at her,
She replies with a smile.

You can see from your window
All the things that I see,
The sunrise and sunset,
And all of it, free.

I see from my window
Whatever I please.
Whatever one looks for,
That is just what one sees.

So please look out your window
And look for a dove,
Let us turn war and strife
Back into love.

Observations

This world and all that's in it,
Was made in just six days.
It all seems like a work of art.
How glorious are His ways.

It really is a great old world,
With all its mistakes and blunders.
For it is full of so many things,
And most of them all wonders.

What is prettier than a sunset,
With its many shades of pinks?
Did you ever stand and watch it,
Just before it sinks?

What is prettier than a sunrise,
As it pops up in the east?
Or a rainbow full of promise,
To say a storm has ceased?

The mountains in their majesty,
Stand towering toward the sky.
No artist can create one,
Though many of them try.

Of all the flowers growing,
What is sweeter than a rose?
Could IBM make one,
Do you suppose?

All about us everywhere,
The dark green ivy vine.
If we could call it orchid,
We would think it fine.

Trees are one of our blessings.
They don't spring up in a day.
And only God can make them,
That is what I hear folks say.

Yes, trees are really beautiful,
And we have so very many.
Can you ever imagine
Your town without any?

And we have so many to choose from,
The linden, maple, oak and pine.
The redwoods are the oldest,
And tallest that you'll find.

The oceans are beautiful and blue,

There is no other way to think it.

So wondrous to behold,

But so salty no one can drink it.

The blowing, billowing wheat field

Is very interesting to see.

It means food for foreign countries,

As well as for you and me.

A bright flash of lightning,

And then a clap of thunder,

Can anybody do it?

Only God, I have to wonder.

Our church steeples are inspiring.

They seem to call to you.

Sometimes I think they say,

Step right into my pew.

Oh, I can't forget the birds.

They sing the live-long day.

They seem to understand each other,

We wish we knew what they say.

Sometimes I call beautiful

A cemetery well kept.

Memories of ones resting there,
And for them so many wept.

It all seems so restful,
I'm sure there are no complaints.
Their troubles are all over,
They are resting with the Saints.

Let us hope 100 years from now,
All wars on earth will cease.
All people will be brothers,
And the world be full of peace.

Old Age

Sometimes I wonder why I'm living.
How did I get so old?
God must have a reason,
At least that's what I'm told.

Old age comes so slowly.
One hardly knows it's here.
But one just gets so wobbly,
As one adds another year.

A year isn't very long,
If you take it day by day.
The little things one still can do,
Helps keep old age at bay.

One does not mind the wrinkles,
Nor even mind the gray hairs.
What we like to think of most,
Is to know that someone cares.

Getting near the century mark
Has its problems, too.
Whether your years were good or bad,
Depends on your point of view.

Well I am going to keep on living,
And enjoy life while it's here.
Knowing I have lots of friends,
And all of them sincere.

And when that last day comes,
And all my work is done.
I will slip away, out of sight of all,
Like a setting sun.

True Riches

Who would you be, if you weren't yourself?
Let's play the game for a while.
Would you be just a common man?
Or would you live in style?

For you can be most anything,
If you want to real, real bad.
But it might turn out to be
Worse than what you had.

Who wants to be a Johnson?
With all his pomp and glory,
Without help from others,
His would be another story.

We could be a Johnson,
And have a "Ladybird."
He once was very humble,
At least that's what I heard.

Now look at all his millions,
Fifty-five million, so they say.
And friends, now I tell you,
That isn't hay.

Now Robert Taylor* started humble,

He was like me and you.

But he reached what he was after,

As only do a few.

Abe Lincoln was also humble.

A noble man was he.

After many struggles,

He set the people free.

When you achieve the White House,

You can't say it was luck.

No, it was perseverance,

And an awful lot of pluck.

You can't get to the top of the ladder

If you always lay in bed.

No, it takes pep and grit and ambition,

If we want to get ahead.

Most anyone can do it,

But you can't sit down and cry.

If you want to obtain a fortune,

You have to try and try.

Riches aren't always money,

Even if they have worth.
Love and friends and a heart of kindness
Are the richest things on earth.

You can't take money with you,
But you can take lots of love.
And you will be rewarded
In the blessed home above.

With riches come great worries,
You worry night and day,
Lest someone get it from you,
It has always been that way.

It is better to be happy,
And let your gains be small.
I would rather be contented,
And have no wealth at all.

Forget the Johnsons and the others,
And think of Peter and Paul,
Who lived a life so devoted,
It should be a pattern for us all.

Let us turn our backs on riches.
Let us be of some great worth.

Let us try to do for others,
And the betterment of earth.

As we serve, we prosper,
And as we work, we grow.
Be good and you will be happy,
The Bible tells us so.

Did you say that you want honor?
You can have it if you do.
You must always walk uprightly.
All things will come to you.

This I believe with all my heart,
Both for you and me:
Of all our blessings here on earth,
The best ones are for free.

*Hollywood actor and Nebraska native (1911-1969).

Tasteless Coffee

As you have your toast and coffee,
Each morning by yourself,
You're kind of like a good book,
Discarded on a shelf.

You once mingled with others.
Now you are out of date.
Like a race horse running,
But came in too late.

You once were somebody,
But not anymore.
You may count a little,
But not high on the score.

You get up each morning
And put the coffee on to brew.
Then look at the paper,
To see who is who.

Next you call up a neighbor,
To hear what is new.
The rest of the day,
You just sit and stew.

The reason is this:
You have lived for too long.
You are really no good,
Like an out-dated song.

You are a little hard of hearing,
Can't hear all they say.
So they leave you alone,
It seems the best way.

They see you have shelter
And plenty to eat.
But as you grow older,
You need more than meat.

You don't say you are lonesome.
You don't want them to know.
But you are a bit weary,
And you miss the folks so.

You could tell them a plenty,
But to keep still is an art,
And to not tell your feelings
Is where you are smart.

You want to be noticed,

Just a kind word or two.
Your days would seem shorter,
Much happier, too.

As I said at the start,
An old book on the shelf,
And a horse too old for running,
Makes me think of myself.

The Changing World

The horse and buggy days are gone.
They were the good old days.
But as the years went by,
People had to change their ways.

The old hitching post is gone.
No more need for those.
Nor can you anymore,
Tell country folks by their clothes.

A parking lot on every corner,
Gas stations everywhere.
Parking meters wherever you look,
And nothing for free, I swear.

Trucks as big as box cars,
Thundering down Main Street.
So many and so dangerous,
We wish they would retreat.

The traffic has become a problem,
Cars racing here and there.
It makes you think you better
Stop, and say a prayer.

When traffic is bad,

Or a train is near,

The driver, so careless,

Seems to have no fear.

All he wants is to pass,

No matter how fast they go.

They never see the sign ahead,

In big letters, it says, "Slow."

The four-lane highway

Takes the place of gravel.

It makes it nicer

For faster travel.

Then the freeways were built.

Now the interstate,

The newspapers and TV,

All the accidents relate.

The accidents are awful,

Getting worse every day.

The loss is not in dollars,

But with human lives they pay.

What to do about it?

No one seems to know.
Everybody has to hurry,
No one will go slow.

Yes, times have changed,
That we can't deny.
But to bring the old days back,
Would any of you try?

No, just step on the gas,
Alas and alack!
We will get started,
But we may not get back!

Wistful Thinking

Backward turn backward,
Oh time in your flight.
Make me a girl again,
Just for one night.

What would I do,
And where I would go?
One thing I tell you,
It wouldn't be slow.

I'd go to a show,
And go to a dance,
How I would hot foot
And how I would prance.

I'd go to a casino
And sit on the plush.
I'll tell you right now,
I'd make them all blush.

I'd turn out the lights.
I would find me a throne.
And you can believe
That I won't be alone.

I would find me a guy

As lonesome as me.

We would turn things wide open,

And sure have us a spree.

We wouldn't be bashful.

We would just sit and spoon.

We would sit and hold hands,

And look at the moon.

We might have a fling,

Or any old thing,

And if he should get a little flip,

We might end up on Sunset Strip.

That is where our young folks go,

There they learn all there is to know.

We would dance the frug* and the bunny

And hop to and fro.

And then we would go

Inside and dine.

Food, you know,

Is where I shine.

Along toward morning,

Home we would go,
Feeling like heck,
Me and my beau.

I am all wrong,
Time doesn't turn back.
For a moment I
Was on the wrong track.

So I will turn about,
And obey the rule.
I will try to be content
With Sunday school.

*A dance craze of the mid-1960s.

Wondering Why

I wonder, yes I wonder,
What life is all about.
Why folks do this and that,
It all is strange, no doubt.

Twinkle, twinkle little star,
Way up there in the sky.
You up there and me down here,
I often wonder why.

I wonder about so many things.
It is hard to keep them straight.
I'm sure I will know some day,
But I can hardly wait.

Why is there a face in the moon?
And why is the sun so hot?
Some say there is life on Mars,
But I say there is not.

They say the world is round,
And that sounds foolish, too.
They have no way to prove it,
So I say it isn't true.

I wonder how the clouds make rain,

And where does the sun go at night?

And why is the rain so wet?

And why is the snow so white?

Why does the sun rise in the east?

And why does it set in the west?

Now there is a puzzle for you,

Who can answer it best?

I wonder why the stars don't fall,

And why they shine so bright,

And if they rest in daytime,

And just come out at night.

Why don't butterflies make butter?

And why do roosters crow?

And when it's hot in summer,

Why do the west winds blow?

Why do men seek riches?

And why do they want to fly?

Is it because the world is restless?

Is that the reason why?

Why do we count our calories, and try to get so thin?

After all the misery is over,
We are just as we have always been.

Why do we get weary?
And all our steps less bold?
Surely the reason cannot be,
That we are getting old.

As I sit here musing,
I wonder why I do.
I should be out there somewhere,
Learning something new.

Why do old folks wrinkle,
Like a dried up prune?
Some of us have already,
The rest of you will soon.

What about the bees and birds?
Is that a question bold?
Are there things that I don't know yet?
That I never have been told?

Now I'm going to quit my worry
About all the hows and whys.
No one knows everything,

So I'm not even going to try.

When you learn the answers,
Please pass them on to me.
I will know as much as you do,
From my worry I'll be free.

Why do we grow so weary
As our time marches by?
We stop and rest and sit and think
Will we never more be spry?

Why can't we live life over,
And have a second try?
How different we would live it,
I'm sure both you and I.

Death cuts down our loved ones,
Who we no more can see.
It seems so sad and needless,
Why oh why does have to be?

This world is such a puzzle,
That is why I keep asking WHY.
I guess we will only understand it,
In the sweet bye and bye.

Religion and Church

Church Revival

Gone is the week of our revival.
We will be with George no more.
He surely tried hard to direct us
To our Home on the other shore.

We will call it Life Renewal,
We pray it will prove to be,
And that we can be more like Him,
And from our sins be free.

May it bring us a little closer
As each day passes by,
And be more as He wants us,
And we can if we will try.

May this week of prayers and witness
Bring us closer to the Throne, and
Help us realize more fully,
That we shall know as we are known

Wrong judgment and fault finding

Are all such little things,
But the Bible says they're sinful
And like a viper stings.

Our church is like one big family,
This saying I hope is true.
You know it only can be,
It all depends on me and you.

George taught us what our church is.
He says it's me and you.
So let us always pull together,
And not leave it to a few.

If we sing and pray together,
And again when we're apart,
I'm sure the Lord will lead us,
And that will be our start.

We know our church is handsome,
Yes, it is very nice.
But nothing comes for free,
Always there is a price.

Now let that price be our devotion,
To God and church be true.

I'm sure He will reward us,
With whatever reward is due.

The days are closing in on us,
We do not have much time.
As He gives us sunset and sunrise,
Let us make each day sublime.

Then as He calls us homeward,
And to our "Heavenly Rest,"
May each of us be ready,
To live with all the blessed.

We shall reap if we faint not,
The Bible tells us so.
So let us be up and doing,
And help to fight the foe.

Satan is just around the corner,
Trying to make us stumble,
To make us vain and worldly,
But God says we must be humble.

We have so many blessings,
All coming from above:
Love and life and happiness,

But the greatest of all is "love."

Our minister can't do it all.
Put your shoulder to the wheel.
Let him know just where you stand,
And also how you feel.

We could make this church a blessing,
A place of influence and renown.
One we all would be proud of,
And a credit to our town.

When Gabriel blows his trumpet
On that wonderful last day,
May each of us all be there,
And we will if we but pray.

We shall live with Him forever,
What a glory that will be.
Across that celestial river,
And all our loved ones, faces see.

Yes, a speedy church renewal
Is really what we need.
We better be up and doing,
And with God's help we will succeed.

Satan is ever after us,

Trying to pull us down.

God says "I am your Maker.

With me, ye shall wear a crown."

You may say this isn't true,

But this is on the level.

As far as taking chances,

Never bargain with the devil.

Easter

E is for the Early church service as we seek our Lord.

A is for Atonement if you pray real hard.

S is for Savior, yours He will be. You have to but ask Him so try it
and see.

T is for Treasures in your Bible to seek. He loves everyone, yes even the
weak.

E is for Entering into the joys of the Lord, verily I promise you will have
your reward.

R is for Records, He keeps one of you. May your name be there and I hope
mine will be, too.

EASTER—Resurrection, Glorious Day. It is for us all, He has shown us the
way.

Religion Retrospect

Give me that old time religion,
It isn't like that anymore.
If you shouted "Amen" in church,
They would throw you out the door.

It was quiet in the sanctuary,
We used to kneel to pray.
Everything was quiet and holy,
It isn't like that today.

I often think of our forefathers,
The way they used to do.
They sang right from their hearts,
And they really meant it too.

Today it is so different,
And so much is red tape,
With apathy and indifference,
People are just about half awake.

Yes, people still go to church,
They sit there in the pew.
But really serious minded,
There are only just a few.

The lofty ring of the old church bell,

Telling me to come.

I think it meant much more to me,

Than it ever did to some.

My little church had no carpet,

And we got along just fine.

It had no parlor or kitchen,

That little old church of mine.

But inside those doors came a feeling,

No other place you felt,

As you ambled down that aisle,

And at your pew you knelt.

I'm so thankful for my memory,

And that I remember still,

That good old-time religion,

In that little church on the hill.

There were prayer meetings Wednesday evenings.

I wonder where they went.

Children went to Sunday school,

They didn't have to be sent.

In church kids paid attention,

We knew we better had.
As we sat there so sober,
Between our mom and dad.

We couldn't play on Sunday,
We couldn't go to shows.
What kids do and where they go
Anymore, nobody knows.

We were taught to be modest,
Where is modesty today?
We were taught to be polite,
And not with smear words play.

Late every Saturday night,
In the old washtub,
We all got our scrubbing,
And a homemade soap back rub.

Then we were ready for Sunday,
All of us climbed the stairs,
And we all crawled into bed
After mother heard our prayers.

Mothers were home those days,
That is something different, too.

I liked those good old days,
And I imagine so did you.

Sunday was a special day.
We all had peace and quiet.
But now it's like all other days,
From a picnic to a riot.

Our churches were not fancy,
No they were plain and small.
But every Sunday morning,
They seemed to hold us all.

Things have changed a lot
In the last 100 years.
If our forefathers saw it now,
They would be in tears.

The world needs a big awakening,
It must get back to God.
Heed the things He tells us,
And tread the roads He trod.

I feel sorry for folks today.
They are missing such a lot.
If things keep on, I think,

The world will go to pot.

God once destroyed a wicked world.

He can do the same again.

I am afraid He will do that,

If it gets too full of sin.

The Bible

The Bible is a precious book
How often do you take a look?

There are verses for the young and some for the old.
Many lessons to be learned and they are good as gold.

It will help you every day,
And help you learn to better pray.

It will help you through tomorrow,
And lighten almost any sorrow.

It tells about the Savior's birth,
And how He came to save this earth.

And if you believe its creed,
Sit right down and begin to read.

The New Church

Our church was getting old.
Also quite a bit too small.
In only a few more years,
It wouldn't hold them all.

The church board called a meeting.
What were they to do?
Could they raise the money,
And build them something new?

First we must find a location,
One to suit us all.
Perhaps we could get started,
And finish it yet this fall.

"I will help all I can,"
Came from quite a number.
"If we all chip in and help,
We soon can buy the lumber."

Where to get our money,
Was our first concern.
The Bible says give 10%
Of everything you earn.

And when we get discouraged,
And feel a bit depressed,
We can always turn to
Our WSCS*.

Our beautiful windows
We wanted to keep,
So we had them made over,
But it wasn't cheap.

By working and giving
And praying some, too,
We now have a church
That's excelled by few.

We all can now sit
On a soft padded pew,
As we offer our thanks
And our vows we renew.

Thanks to Rev. Ed
For all that you do.
For your manual labor,
And your good sermons, too.

Just working together

Is all that it took.

We got our guidance,

From the Blessed Book.

May the works of our God,

Proclaimed by our "Friar,"

Lead us all onward,

Till He calls us up higher.

-----written for son Gerald's church in Albany, Illinois

*Women's Society of Christian Service.

Words of Advice

A Graduate

Now when you get to college,
Try to cram in lots of knowledge,
Because you will need all you can get
If you want to travel in the upper set.

Four long years are ahead of you,
No use in saying it, you already know.
Five days each week you toe the mark,
And on weekends, go on a lark.

Once a week write to your ma.
On special occasions, write to your pa.
That is where you get your money,
So it's up to you to keep them sunny.

All your teachers you must obey,
And in the long run it will pay.
Listen to me and don't you fret,
You may get to be the teacher's pet.

So watch your step and be real good,

And only do the things you should.

After four long years of toil and strife,

You may find yourself a wife.

Look them over, one and another,

And we hope you find one like your mother.

-----written for a friend's son

Be Thankful

Be thankful, Oh be thankful,
An American you are.
You could live in Russia
Or in China, clear away so far.

Be thankful you are not colored*
And that your face is white,
And that we don't have a war here,
And all of us have to fight.

Be thankful you are a Christian,
And to a lovely church belong,
And that you are able to go there
And even help them sing a song.

Be thankful for this lovely day,
Instead of cold and snow,
And that you have good shelter,
When 'ere the north winds blow.

Be thankful for so many things,
Count them one by one.
It surely will surprise you
When your day is done.

Be thankful for a useful life,
That you had work to do.
That you had health and faith and hope,
And they have helped you through.

And I do give Him thanks today,
For all that I have had.
For health and wealth and happiness,
And so little has been sad.

Be thankful for our churches.
Where would we be today,
If we didn't have them,
Where we meet and sing and pray.

Be thankful for your parents,
Who helped you on your way,
Who sacrificed and worked for you,
And taught you how to pray.

Yes, thank them every day
And thank them every night,
That they were so very good to you,
And your life turned out all right.

Be most thankful for many friends.

We have them if we try,

And if we thought we didn't have,

I'm sure we would want to die.

*The editor truly believes that this line was written because blacks were being treated badly, not because of racism.

Now is the Time

If you are ever going to love me,
Even just a little bit,
Let me know it while I'm living,
So I can treasure it.

If you have a word of kindness,
Now is the time to let me know.
I am waiting now to hear it,
So say it now before I go.

I'll not feel your kind caresses,
When grass grows above my face.
I'll not feel your loving kindness,
In my last low resting place.

To chisel words on marble,
Or write them on a slate,
Will be no help to a loved one,
For then it will be too late.

Winning the Race

Life is just a vicious cycle.
We are either good or bad.
We can either make someone happy,
Or just as easily make them sad.

Yes, life is so like a puzzle.
Nothing counts as much as love.
Let us give it out to others,
As we receive it from above.

True to self is the beginning,
The next step will find a way.
The Bible says to love your neighbor,
And we must always watch and pray.

Let us try to keep life peaceful,
For the peaceful shall be blest.
Tired and wary if we faint not,
We are told we shall find rest.

As we travel ever onward,
Can we make this life sublime?
And in so doing can we leave
Footprints on the sands of time?

The time has come for me to say
That I am growing old.
My steps are slow, and there are
Silver hairs among the gold.

Time is short for seniors,
Our race is almost run.
We better get right busy,
And have ourselves some fun.

Our fun is what we make it,
And it isn't any sin.
So let's be up and doing,
Before time closes in.

So friends, here is a warning:
What 'ere you plan to do,
Get busy and get at it,
Your days here, might be few.

I always have been active,
Ever since I was born.
I'm going to keep on doing,
Until Gabriel blows his horn.

Then I will tell Mr. Gabriel,

Sir, I have done my best.
I hope that he will answer:
Enter in with all the blessed.

But if he doesn't—oh mercy.
Just think what he could say.
My friend you are not ready,
Come back another day.

We must be ready for our summons,
Because it is sure to come.
It will be good news if you're lucky,
But otherwise for some.

The Bible is our guidepost.
We all know that quite well.
So choose your destination,
It is either Heaven or -----

If you want to be successful,
If you really want to win,
Get out there and roll up your sleeves,
Hard work is not a sin.

Sin is being naughty,
And it is so easy to do.

Easy at least for me,
Maybe it isn't for you.

When this life is over,
And our race is run,
He will say come up higher,
And will say to each of us, "well done."

And as we pass over Jordan,
To that bright land above,
He will say "Well done my servant,
Enter in with those you love."

Wise Words

Do not look for wrong or evil,
It is ever at your side.
It takes less time to look for good,
Than from the evil hide.

Such small words can make trouble,
And so unintentionally, too.
You and I have said them
So carelessly, 'tis true.

Don't carry a chip on your shoulder,
It will save you many a tear.
The chip will only hurt you,
And others, too, I fear.

Shut your eyes to little insults,
They can hurt when not intended.
They break a heart and sting like bees,
And some friend may be offended.

Speak nicely, if you speak at all,
So many hearts are sad.
They may need a word of kindness,
Just a few words could make them glad.

Yes, be glad that you are living
In a world where you can smile,
And soon you will be thinking
Life really is worthwhile.

Love is our first commandment,
It ties in with all the others.
If we understand correctly,
We are all sisters and brothers.

So look for a rainbow,
It is always there to see,
And it ever holds a promise,
You know, for you and me.

Let us trudge along together
And all commandments keep.
Then as we end life's journey,
We will have no need to weep.

Life is what we make it,
We all know this is true.
As much as you give others,
Twice that much comes back to you.

A smile takes just a second,

A frown takes two or three.
You have a choice of either,
Which will your choice be?

We are in for something different,
We are going to take a fall,
If we don't have a reformation,
It is going to get us all.

As time goes on we realize,
That we cannot live alone.
With so much sadness around us,
Our time is not our own.

With others we must share our time.
We must learn to give and take.
As we give we also get,
And a better world we make.

Let us not shirk our duties,
Let us reach out a little more.
Lend a helping hand to others,
Or mend a heart that is sore.

When you are not too busy,
And you stop to rest awhile,

Think of something pleasant,
And a frown will become a smile.

One smile is like good medicine,
Two is like a cure.
Three will help most anything,
Of that you may be sure.

There is an old saying:
To thine own self be true,
And the better things in life,
Will surely follow you.

We were put here to be happy,
So happy let us be.
Let our life be full of love,
For love you know is free.

This life is swiftly passing into Eternity.
If His love is in our hearts,
I'm sure His face we will see.

So altogether we are striving
For that land so bright and fair.
And when at last He calls you,
May we all be gathered there.

Miscellaneous

Flowers and Spring

We all love our beautiful flowers.
How could we have them without showers?
And who sends the showers from above?
We all know it is our God of love.

Roses and daisies and violets blue,
Tulips and jonquils and hyacinths, too.
Pansies and lilies and lilacs so nice,
All bloom in season, smelling of spice.

The leaves and the grass so welcome in spring,
Make us happy and make the birds sing.
All nature about us seems to thrive,
And we are so happy that we are alive.

Spring in her glory all dressed in her best,
Wakes up from her long, cold winter's rest.
The buds are all bursting, will soon be in bloom,
And summer is coming, it can't be too soon.

So enjoy each day as it comes along,

And be like the birds and burst forth in song.

This little maxim I wish to impart:

You will always be happy with spring in your heart.

Order of the Eastern Star

Order of the Eastern Star,*
Related to the Masons are.
They both are known throughout the earth,
Centuries ago they had their birth.

To be a member is like a band,
Encircling one another.
So at all times we feel like
We are sister and brother.

The Worthy Matron is in the east,
With a gavel in her hand.
And next beside her sits
The Worthy Patron Grand.

Eighteen officers in each chapter,
And change office every year.
Some elected, some appointed,
For their matron work with cheer.

We have a right to pick and choose,
Just one requirement is a must.
We cannot be too worldly,
And in one God we must trust.

171

Eastern Star is a wonderful order.

We have heroines five.

We are supposed to emulate them,

And so for this we strive.

First there is Adah, her heart very heavy,

Determined to die in the right.

Went up in the mountains to pray,

For strength to do what was right.

Ruth was a fair young damsel.

She loved her mother-in-law.

They were gleaners in the field,

Gathering barley and straw.

Esther queen upon her throne,

With her scepter bright.

Asked a favor of her king,

And he granted her what was right.

Martha who was full of faith,

Found her brother dead.

She asked the Lord to help her,

And she believed all that He said.

Electa, a pagan converted,

Would not trample the cross.
She stood by her convictions,
Although she suffered the loss.

Thus we have the daughter
And the widows sign.
The wife and sister and mother,
All of them sublime.

These virtues of our heroines,
Should adorn our lives.
Make us true to our convictions,
For a better life to strive.

We pledge allegiance to our flag,
Long may it ever wave.
May He who doeth all things well,
Keep us ever brave.

A musician is quite important,
As we have a beautiful drill,
And it makes the work more lovely,
As music always will.

As we go forth into the world,
Not knowing what might be,

Look for His star in the east,

For He will take care of thee.

*A fraternal order based on the teachings of the Bible, open to both women and men of all religious faiths.

Pills

If there is anything
That makes me ill,
It's to hear so much
About the pill.

In every paper
And on every page,
You see the ads.
It is all the rage.

In every store
And on every shelf,
You know it's there.
You can help yourself.

Take them in the morning,
Or take them at night.
Take two or three and
They make everything right.

Don't get me wrong.
They are white and thin.
What I'm saying here
Is take aspirin!

www.ingramcontent.com/pod-product-compliance
Lightning Source LLC
Chambersburg PA
CBHW020948030426
42339CB00004B/5